Also by John Yamrus

One Step at a Time
78 RPM
Keep The Change
New And Used
Start To Finish
Someone Else's Dreams (novel)
Something
Poems
Those
Coming Home
American Night
15 Poems
Heartsongs
Lovely Youth (novel)
I Love

Blue Collar

new poems
by
John Yamrus

PublishAmerica
Baltimore

© 2006 by John Yamrus.
All rights reserved. No part of this book may be reproduced, stored in a retrieval system or transmitted in any form or by any means without the prior written permission of the publishers, except by a reviewer who may quote brief passages in a review to be printed in a newspaper, magazine or journal.

First printing

At the specific preference of the author, PublishAmerica allowed this work to remain exactly as the author intended, verbatim, without editorial input.

ISBN: 1-4241-4017-X
PUBLISHED BY PUBLISHAMERICA, LLLP
www.publishamerica.com
Baltimore

Printed in the United States of America

For Kathy

Introduction

by RD Armstrong

    In a world that is hell-bent on gobbling itself up, the poetry of John Yamrus is a welcome break from all this great crashing about and railing against all that is wrong. The poems in this collection have an easy comfort to them. I realize that sounds trite and I certainly don't mean to trivialize John's work. In the broad spectrum of poetry, a crazy patchwork quilt of styles and themes at best, those who notice, much less capture, the everyday matters of the heart are, to me, a rare breed. Sure, we all must rage against the light at some point, but that's not all there is. Most of the time it's just little events that seemingly dull the senses, yet it's these very moments that are the glue that holds the whole mess together. How we deal with this really says who we are.

    Reading these poems one is touched by the overall matter-of-factness of them; this is not to say that they are bland by any means. Each poem is a statement. Factual or not, each poem presents its case, without all the emotional hoopla that is so fashionable these days. Yamrus writes from the gut without sensationalizing it. He isn't sentimental or sappy. The poems have an understated simplicity, even when the themes have an edge. There are no big "Hollywood" endings here. No swelling up of the music cueing us to feel this way or that. No, these poems celebrate the simple, sometimes quiet, moments. The *sitting in the backyard, listening to the hiss as twilight approaches* moments.

The moments of peace spent with your dog or your woman or your car that crop up between the great crashing "really important" moments...

Living in post 9-11 America, it has become increasingly difficult to separate the trees from the forest, so to speak. While it's the poet's job to tell the story, these days the story is clouded with erroneous information. The poet's maturity and craft determines how well he or she does it. Fanfare and melodrama may be entertaining, but for my money, I prefer the hard-working poets who labor quietly away from the daily hubbub. There will always be time to rage against injustice and whatever the cause-of-the-day is. That barricade is ably manned. But we mustn't forget the human element, either. John Yamrus succeeds in doing this in a quiet and uncompromising way.

RD Armstrong
Long Beach, CA

RD Armstrong lives and works near the Los Angeles harbor, "where the work gets done". He is the publisher of the Lummox Journal, one of the best kept secrets in the small press to date. His latest book, which he edited and contributed to, is LAST CALL: The Legacy of Charles Bukowski; which was voted "Best Poem Anthology – 2005" by Muses Review. www.lummoxpress.com

Blue Collar

in your life

if you
get to be
your absolute
most crystal
perfect best,

even once,

you
have

won.

twice

this wet
and rainy summer
we got water in the basement
and i ended up
working
all night
to keep things dry.

tonight,
for the third time
it's coming in again.

it's 3:43 in the morning
and
it's coming in again.

only
right now
i'm sitting here
and taking a break.

i've got a can of soda
that i'm going to finish
and i'm also
going to read
at least a chapter or two
of Proust.

y'see,
i've come to the conclusion
that no matter what happens…

no matter how little
i work,

or how
hard i work,

sooner or later
the water
will dry up,

while Proust
never
will.

it was

a brown house
with a wide porch.

the Connor's lived there.

when i was a kid
Tommy and i
used to hide
behind the
swing
and whistle
at the girl next door.

her house
was white aluminum siding
and her name was Annie.

her father worked nights
in the RCA factory
and she was
dating this guy
who looked
like Elvis.

he drove a white
Chevy
and would pick her up
on Friday nights.

Tommy and i
would scrunch down
behind the swing
and whistle
and laugh
when she looked over.

we thought
we were cool
and we knew
she was hot.

and we'd
whistle again.

eventually,
the days passed,
the summer ended
and we gave it up.

what we did then,
nearly 50 years ago,
was no joke…

although
we will all
go to our graves
trying to
get it.

sooner or later

it catches
up with you.

no matter
how well
you run
the race,
it catches up with you
and you're left
standing alone,
blindfolded,
with your back
against the wall
as the guy
at the other end of the yard
starts counting down…

"Ready…"

the only thing that matters
as he continues
to count…

"Aim…"

the only thing in the world
that's left to you
is to hold your head
high
and face the

"*Fire!*".

i ask

the lady poet
"what are you
doing now?
what's your
ambition?"

and
she says
"i want to write.
i know i've got
great poems,
even immortal poems
in me."

"and what
are you
doing about it?"

"oh,
i'm reading
everything i can

preparing myself.

getting
the instrument
ready."

and i say
"yes,
but are you
writing?"

"no.
i'm not
ready for that yet.

i'm waiting
till the time's right.

waiting
for the proper
inspiration.

do you
understand?"

yes, ma'am,
i'm afraid
i do.

"you're not very funny"

she said.
and i was
too tired
to tell her
i was too tired
to be funny.

so, we lay there,
side by side,
in the sun,
listening to the music
from the yard next door.

it was a jazz station
and not very good
and not very clear.

but,
it didn't matter.

we were both
half asleep.

besides,
sometimes
a grimace
is
almost
as good as a
grin.

there has to be

an end to
toothaches
and headaches…

and hemorrhoids
and pimples.

there has to be
an end
to jobs with no heart
and people
with no soul.

there has to be
an end
to all the
tiny
little pains
that wear you down
and leave you sick
and staring at the wall
at 3 a.m.
on a Saturday night.

there has to be.

but,
i don't

see it.

now that Bukowski's dead

what are all the
wanna-be's
that never were
going to do?

what are they
going to do
for inspiration?

who are they
going to
turn to?

who's going to tell them
how to drink,
think
or write?

who's going to tell them
that Dostoyevsky's cool…

that John Fante
had a way
with words

and that it's
a lot more fun
to stay in bed
and think about it
than it is
to have to

get up
and
write about it?

now,
they'll
pick his bones
like they did
with all the others
and look for reasons
where there were
none…

and explanations
where there are
none…

where (more often
than not) there's just
some slob
who lived his life
and wrote
and loved
and slept
and ate
and died.

there's
no mystery,
really…

just
ask
Bukowski.

i remember it was 1964

and my whole family
had driven
in the Dodge
to New Jersey
to visit this former
neighbor of ours
who had retired
and gone to live
with his children.

back then
a trip like that
was a real
adventure.

i remember
the car being
crammed with maps
and food and
blankets and
toys, and
me and my sister
sat in the back
counting license plates
and cheering
every time
the old Dodge
got up enough steam
to pass another car.

it was a
Saturday.

a bright and
wonderful
Saturday.

i remember
getting there
and meeting their kids
and not quite liking
their son.

he was about my age,
skinny,
with buck teeth and
red hair
and freckles.

we ate
hamburgers
in the yard
and they had
this green
flowered swing
and the radio was on
and it played
Nat Cole's
new song
which was the big hit
that year.

all things considered,
it was a great day.

our parents sang,
told stories
and rocked in the swing,

while we kids
played
and fought
on the floor...

wrestling,
sweating
and
finally
crying.

the next morning
we got up early,
had breakfast
and drove back home,
looking (in my
mind's eye)
for all the world
like that
Norman Rockwell
painting...

just
another family
riding in a car.

the next year
my father was dead
and the whole world
had changed,
leaving me

(for the rest of my life)
just another
skinny kid,
alone
on a summer night
looking
for a
fight.

i always figured i'd end up

being
the crazy one.

on
the street,

walking around
waving my arms at passing cars,
with hair down to my shoulders,

wearing high top sneakers
and carrying 3 ballpoint pens
and one finely sharpened pencil
in the pocket of my shirt.

i always figured that
was going to be me.

but today
i saw him.

the man i wanted
to be.

he had the hair and the shirt
and the pencil and the pens.

he even had on
a pair of wild plaid pants
and a black and white
striped shirt.

he's The Man...

he's a God...

he's a miracle in a pony tail
and 8 dollar shoes.

and here i am,
powerless,
barely able
to describe him
as he
picks his nose
and walks
away.

the lady writer

wrote this article
about me.

in it
she says
we recently
went out for drinks
and talked about
"the current state
of American literature".

no big deal, really…

except
it never happened.

not one word
of it.

i don't know
why she wrote it.

i'm certainly
not that interesting.

my conversation skills
are non-existant.

i am not
a fascinating guy.

anyway,
if you happen to read her article,
what'll tip you off
that it's made up
is the fact
that i couldn't care less
about the current state
of anybody's literature
and wouldn't be caught dead
talking about it.

so, to you, ma'am –
the next time
you feel the need
to write about
us having
an imaginary conversation
and imaginary drinks…

remember this:

it's
your turn
to buy.

the poems weren't

working.
i felt drained…
hot…
dry…
useless…

there was nothing
for me to do
but
go out in the yard
and listen to
the fat bald guy
who lives in the back
fighting with his wife.

i couldn't make out
most of what they said
except when
she called him
"a damn fool
for being normal".

on that point
i had to
agree with her.

if i were a gentleman
i would have stood
just then
and thanked her
for giving me
this poem.

but
i didn't.

i just lay there,
listening,
while the dogs of the world barked
and doors slammed
and order
was finally
restored.

i was just now

thinking about
this friend of mine
who has cancer.

i ran into her
the other day.

she was in her back yard
having a smoke
and i was at the house
next to hers,
banging on the door,
when i saw her.

i shouted over
and said
"hey, Evelyn!
how are you?
you're looking pretty good!
how do you feel?"

she took a great big
drag on her smoke,
looked at me
and said

"violated"

and walked
inside.

i wasn't expecting that.

i had wanted her to say
"fine".

i wanted to hear
"peachy keen"
and "dandy".

i've known Evelyn
for 40 years.

i knew her way back when she
used to lay in the yard
in her two piece
bathing suit.

she was pretty then.

even beautiful.

sometimes,
the most unexpected thing
about beauty

is
finding it
gone.

i was stopped at a light today

i had
Stevie Wonder
on the radio.

i wasn't
bothering anyone.
i was just
stopped at a light
and listening to my music.

just as the light turned green
a couple of kids
walked out in front of me,
walking real slow…

staring at me…

almost daring me
to hit them.

i stared back,
rolled the window down
and turned Little Stevie up
REAL LOUD.

i thought to myself:
"all right, tough guy.
i'll let you pass
this time.

go ahead…

you have
my permission…

enjoy your season in the sun.
it's shorter than you think."

then
the light changed…

i hung my skinny arm
out the window,

flipped them the bird
and drove on down the line.

i'll tell you

the reason why
i don't read
haiku…

it's not
that i don't
understand,

or
enjoy,

or
appreciate
them.

i do.

it's just
that
every time
i read them,
for weeks afterward,
my poems
end up sounding like:

*the wild singing
of a short old man
standing in an open field.*

see what i mean?

did i ever tell you

about the time Linda
said i was good,
but that i'd never be
Bukowski?

Linda was a poet.

one of Bukowski's
girlfriends
in the '70s.

for a while she edited and published
a pretty decent little magazine.

she wrote to me saying
that she loved my poems...

actually, it's been so long now
i really don't remember
if she loved them
or liked them,
but it doesn't matter...

she said that i was good,
but i would never be great...
because i wasn't
mad.

Bukowski (she said) was mad...
and he was
great.

i wrote back
saying that she was right...
Bukowski IS mad
and Bukowski IS great,
but if one of the qualifications
for being mad
and being great
was having to put up with the likes of her,
then i'd be more than happy
to settle for what i am
and what i'm
going to be.

that was 30 years ago,
and do you know what?

i'm still not mad
and i'm still not
great...

but, every now and then,
when the moon's just right
i'm not
half bad.

Tommy Henry's father

drank.
when i was a kid
he was the janitor
in our school.

he also worked
at the bowling alley next door,
and every Saturday
he'd go on a bender
and tie one on.

i remember
one Saturday
i woke up
hearing somebody
playing "Reveille"
on a bugle.

i ran out
onto the porch
and looked up the street,
and there was
Tommy's father
flat on his back
on the steps
of the bar on the corner,
playing a bugle,
screaming "EVERYBODY UP!
IT'S SATURDAY MORNING!
EVERYBODY UP!"

what a neighborhood
it was.

nobody got upset.
nobody called the cops.

that's just
the way it was.
just old man Henry
playing a bugle
on a Saturday morning.

it was later on
in that same summer
(a summer of daylong
baseball games,
of dew on the grass
and sweat on the
brim of my hat),
...it was that same summer
when he
cut his fingers off.

he was trimming some trees
at the school
and the glove he was wearing
got caught in the chainsaw
and his hand
got pulled across the blade.

i can still hear him laughing,
like Lamont Cranston...
like The Shadow,
laughing
this great,

sad
"mwee-hee-hee…"
as he reached down
and picked his fingers
off the ground.

they were these
little
bloody
sausage things.

after that
he quit drinking,
got diabetes
and never
looked at
the bugle
again.

do you know Pete Gray?

the one arm'd ballplayer?
he played for the St. Louis Browns
in the major leagues
in 1944.

77 games.

234 at bats.

51 hits.

it always killed him
that he was known
as "the one arm'd ballplayer".

people said he was no good.
a freak.
that he only made it to the big leagues
because there was a war on
and all the "normal" guys
were in uniform.

Pete Gray's 87 years old now and lives in the town i grew
up in. i never met the man. he's old and crotchety and
bitter. i hear that if you ask him about his season in the
bigs he'll cuss you out. he wants to be remembered strictly
as a ballplayer, not a curiosity.

and in spite of all that…
on top of all that…
and because of all that…

there's still the
single
unalterable fact
that in 1944,
Hitler's army was on the run,
the world was on the verge of a whole new age
and a guy named Pete Gray
played some baseball

in the bigs.

i made soup

the other night, (i'm a
thoroughly
domesticated animal.
if you
remember to
leave me out
every now and then
i don't even
crap on the rug).

and, for a hoot
i threw in
some alphabet
noodles.

there wasn't
a lot of them,
but enough
at least
to make it
a little more
interesting.

and,
being the seer,
soothsayer
and purveyor
of broken dreams
that i am,
i spent the entire evening
watching tv,

trying to
read my future
in the bottom of
that bowl of
carrots and celery
and peas.

finally,
i gave it up
and went to bed
content in the knowledge
that the future
is
what it is,
and the only thing
any of us
ever has to know
is how to survive
the coming night.

this morning

i deleted a bunch of
poems-in-progress
from the computer.

i had
to do it.

they read like
shit.

not one thing
memorable
about any of them.

they were like
boring wallpaper.

like
elevator music.

so, i deleted them
and wrote to a friend,
telling her what i did
and she called me a jerk,
saying if i was concerned about
saving space on my computer
that i shouldn't be.

i wasn't.

i was concerned about
saving crappy poetry.

and,
if i had any guts,
you wouldn't even
be reading
this.

we were on vacation

in Martinique, and
we were on the beach
on one of those days
that was so bright and beautiful
that you figured
if you ever had to die
this wouldn't be such a bad
day and place
for it.

not bad at all.

anyway,
the beach was crowded.
to my left
were this family of Japanese…
their 3 kids
were so covered in suntan lotion
they looked like
tiny Kabuki.

on the other side,
a little further down,
was this old guy…

maybe 65,
maybe a little bit older.

he looked kind of like
Kirk Douglas at 65
and was in good shape
for a guy his age.

even better than that,

with him were
2 girls who
were maybe 20,
maybe 25...

and every now and then
one of them
would get off her chair
and sit next to him,
rubbing suntan lotion
on his back
and legs.

and he'd lay there,
real cool,
like he deserved
every bit
of what he had.

and i thought
good for you, pop...
maybe you do, and
maybe you don't...

in the long run,
it just doesn't matter,
so why take any chances.

it's a Saturday morning

and
i'm doing laundry.

i take a basket of clothes
to hang out in the yard.

the sun's nice
on my back and arms,
but it's Fall now
and not as warm as it was.

i look over at my garden
and what's left of the tomatoes…
Fall tomatoes…
getting older…
not quite what they used to be.

i take the last sweater off the line,
fold it
and drop it into the basket.

the sun's now lower in the sky,
(just barely over the edge of the fence)
and i pick up the basket
and walk back toward the house.

on the way in
i take one last look
at the tomatoes
and say
"see you later, pal…
i guess we'd better start
getting used to each other".

my contemporaries...

of all the writers
i used to know
way back
when my first books were coming out,
very few are still around...

Allan was in a car crash,
dropped out,
got cancer and died.

Brent is
making his living
writing articles
for cooking magazines.

Moses went back to nature
somewhere in the Arizona desert.

by now
he's probably a
short order cook
in some diner
on route 66.

Michael's a preacher
in Connecticut.

Joe teaches computer.

and Don
one day
just packed up
and disappeared.

no,
of all the guys
i started out with
i'm the only one
not smart enough
to figure out a way
to truly
kick
this habit.

imagine that.

my friend John

died the other day.
he was 82.

he worked hard
all his life
and had the perfect retirement.

golfing all day...
martinis at 5.

after his second drink
he'd start reciting poetry...

mostly Robert W. Service.

stuff he learned
and loved
when he was a kid.

poems he carried with him
all his life.

poems like
"The Cremation Of Sam McGee",
or "The Face On The Barroom Floor".

i can hear him now,
saying:
"There are strange things done
in the midnight sun
by the men
who moil for gold"...

sometimes,
when he couldn't sleep,
he'd lie there,
on his back,
reciting line after line
out loud
and he'd say to Mildred
"I'm sorry to bore you with these.
I know you've heard them before,
but I love them so much".

and she'd kiss his eyes
and she'd kiss his cheek
and they'd fall asleep
aging
and happy
and tired…

dreaming
of Sam McGee.

it's all too safe…

running
with the bulls.

sky
diving.

climbing
Mount Everest.

wrestling
alligators.

racing
cars.

catching bullets
in your teeth.

it's all
too simple.

too
safe.

just once
let one of

those guys
come down here

and try
writing

one
really honest

poem.

this lady at the bank

is the
cleanest person i know.

she's
obsessed with it.

she's always wiping her hands,
using those wipes
from one of those dispensers
she keeps on the shelf
next to her.

this afternoon,
just to drive her nuts,
i placed a crumpled tissue
on the counter
in front of her.

i said: "look,
i found this
on the floor…
i was wondering
if you could
throw it out for me".

i wish
you could have seen her face.

it was like
i just put
a dead rat
on the counter.

she backed up
a couple of steps
then whipped out
a tissue
and covered the thing.

using a piece of paper,
she pushed the pile
into the trash.

then,
she pulled out a spray bottle
and cleaned the counter.

still not finished,
she wiped her hands
TWICE
with the wet wipes.

she offered me one…

to be polite,
i wiped my hands
and handed it back to her.

she wrapped it in another wet wipe
and threw the whole pile out,
saying "There! now we're all clean."

god,
what i wouldn't give
to see what she does
in the bathroom!

but,
all things considered,
there's almost a certain majesty
to her compulsion...

an insane
sort of glory.

the hell with it,
i thought,
we've all got
our own little
peculiarities.

i wonder
what mine are?

then, i picked up my cash,

folded it
neatly,

rotated it
6 times in the air,

touched it to my chin,

put it in my wallet,
face side out,

turned
and walked away.

it's over.

that's it,
it's over.

for years
i always wrote my poems
out of love…

well, maybe not
always out of love…

sometimes
despair
or desperation
or any combination of the three.

but certainly
always out of need.

recently, though,
my books have been selling
a bit better…

and that scares me.

let me explain:
this morning
i was writing an e-mail
to a publisher
and in it i said
*"now that the new book's
done*

*and doing well,
it's time i
get to work on the next."*

GET TO WORK!

on poems?

that settles it...
if i don't do something soon
it'll all be over
and the only thing i'll write
will be grocery lists
and laundry lists
and notes for delivery men.

so, i'm asking you...

do me a favor...

please...

if you're in a bookstore
right now
and you're reading this...
put the book
back on the shelf.

don't buy it.

please.

do it for
me.

do it for
us.

i'll owe you
one.

there's nothing hard about it, really…

you get up in the morning,
drag your feet across
the carpet,
down the hall and
into the bathroom,

making sure to
run the water
in the sink
just long enough
that it
comforts you, but
doesn't
wake you.

then you inspect
the face:
checking it out
for any signs of
ruin,
anger,
resignation,
decay,
or anything else
that might show up
on the prow of the ship
you so proudly
present to the world.

and,
regardless of
whether you
find something there
or not,
you figure
"the heck with it",
dry yourself off
and
start all over again.

Henry Miller,

James Jones,
Dos Passos,
Zola,
Kerouac,
Meyer Levin…

the thing
about it
is
that
they're all dead
and i'm
still here,
fighting with this poem
that won't go away.

the good thing
about it
is
there's beer
in the refrigerator,

books
on the shelf

and
a movie on tv.

that's good enough
for me.

Steinbeck and Zola
and all the rest
can have
their
immortality.

i'm more than content
with what little is left
of mine.

i think there's a moral in here somewhere:

Miller sat
at the end of the dock,
fishing.

i asked him
if he'd caught anything
and he said
"nah,
the tide
ain't right".

so, i said
"if the tide's not right,
why are you
sitting there,
fishing?"

and he said
"sometimes
the tide's right
and sometimes
it's not.

but,
you always
gotta fish."

perfect

it's a few days
before Christmas
and i'm sitting in the sun room
Reading *Doctor Zhivago*.

my dog's
sleeping on the couch next to me.

she's got this thing on her neck
that the vet said
we should keep an eye on.

outside,
it's snowing.

the perfect backdrop
to Zhivago
and his problems
with Lara
and the world.

i always loved that scene
in the movie version
where Omar Sharif
as Zhivago
began writing
his Lara poems…

it's freezing
in the Russian winter
and he's got on
his fingerless gloves.

then,
he wipes off his paper,
prepares his pens
and begins to write.

just then
the music rises
in that memorable theme
and you just *know*
he's writing
the best
and most beautiful
poems ever.

then
i close the book,
put it on the table
at my right
and
look down at my dog.

she's asleep,
with the sun
warming her neck
and her back

and she's stinking her own
peculiar little doggie stink.

i reach down
and scratch her
neck
and notice that the wart
hasn't gotten any bigger.

i look out the window
and see the two of us
reflected in the glass...

perfect.

the phone rings

i try to
ignore it.

i'm busy
with a poem
and can't be bothered.

but,
it keeps on ringing.

"go away!"
i shout,
but it keeps on ringing.

finally,
after about 20 rings,
they give up
and i go back
to the poem.

it's not
a very good poem,
and i sit there,
staring at the phone,
hoping they'll call again.

i have very few friends

and not one of them
cares to discuss
Kerouac,
or Steinbeck
or Pound.

not one of them
has ever read
Under The Volcano,
The Cantos
or *On The Road.*

i like it
that way.

i have
very few friends…
two, or three
or four.

but
each
and every
one of them
is perfectly willing
to sit in the yard
on a Saturday night

with a story
and a song

or, silence
and a beer

and the sun
going down

and the radio
on.

November, 1955

the date has
no particular importance
or significance to me.

it means
nothing.

it popped into my head
because i was just on the computer,
looking at a web site
called The Rockabilly Hall Of Fame.

i saw that date…

November, 1955…
and i didn't
feel the need
to click on it
to see where it took me,
or what it meant…

because
i already knew.

in November, 1955
i was 4 years old
and it was dark already
and my father was
just getting home
from his job in the mines,
driving that old black Dodge
we used to have

and my sister was 9
and my mother was
young.

November, 1955.

i think
it was snowing then.

yeah,
i'm sure it was.

the immortal poem

does not
just
happen.

it's usually
nothing more
than a description
of
a day in a life

and
some days
are just
more interesting
than others.

the other day

i had my yearly
visit to the eye doctor.

they gave me all the tests,
marching me from room to room,
poking,
prodding,
peeking.

eye drops,

air…

they were very thorough.
and the doctor (a
nice enough guy,
in his 50s, who has
a different hair color
every time i see him.

this time it's bright yellow)

changes my prescription.
"just a bit.
we're gonna tweak it" he says.

two weeks later
i pick up the new glasses
and they don't work.

everything's out of shape.

distorted.

i go back in
and the tech says to me
"give it a couple of days.
you'll adjust".

for three days
i was stumbling down steps,
tripping on curbs
and generally acting like
i'd had 4 too many
at 2 in the afternoon.

finally, i went back to their office
and said "look, these don't work.
just give me my old prescription back".

"oh, no! we can't do that.
we're professionals!
we tested you thoroughly and
this is the right prescription."

well, they may be professionals,
but it was still
the wrong prescription.

finally, after a lot of back and forth,
they got it right
and i can see
and walk
and read again…

and this poem
is

my
revenge.

at the funeral

just before
they closed the coffin,
the two girls
noticed something.

they called the undertaker over
and one of them said
"where's her ring?"

the undertaker (who was a woman
in her 40s,
with badly thinning hair
and a
cracked front tooth)
looked into the coffin
and said
"you can't see it.
it's on her bottom hand".

that
should have been the end of it,
but for some reason
they didn't believe her
and one of them
reached into the coffin
and lifted up the hand…

"where's the ring?"

"oh, i must have forgot."

and she walked into the office
and came out
with the ring
and put it back
where it belonged.

she looked at the girls
and walked away,
humming nervously to herself
and pulling at a strand
of her
rapidly thinning hair.

sooner or later,
stealing from the dead
has got to
wear you down.

and the undertaker,
who lived in rooms on the second floor,
went upstairs
and gave her seven year old
a ham sandwich,
a glass of milk
and a dirty
look.

mundane

we sat on the couch
and watched tv,
while you ate
Girl Scout cookies
and i had a beer.

every now and then
one of the dogs
would
yawn.

one of us
would change the station
or get up
to go to the bathroom.

someone once said
that art
is merely
observation.

or, was it
observation
and thoughtful interpretation?

i forget.

anyway,
it was just a typical evening.
we were on the couch
and every now and then
one of us would change the station.

so,
what do you think
about that?

the academic poet

has been included in
countless anthologies.

he's received fellowships
and grants.

he's known to be an activist
and socialist.

he's currently publishing
a long long poem
that's going to run into several volumes,
complete with arcane and obscure references.

at least once a month
he quotes Aeschyles
and Pindar.

he's published several volumes of his
talks and essays.

he's very good at
playing the game.

he's always sure to
shake the right hands.

he's also
never had a hang nail
and his dog's
never thrown up on the rug.

his bills are always paid
and he's never known
what it's like
to have to miss a meal.

his socks always match,
his hair's always combed
and he's never made a fool out of himself
in front of family and friends.

and
his poetry
shows it.

there's no soul,
no guts.

it's so much empty air…

just talk.

when he's gone,
other academics
will discuss his life
and dissect his books.

people will forget.

and other academics
will take his place.

and others
will soon take theirs.

i'm afraid
there will always be
academics,

smiling, confident
and sure.

and this
is just
one more reason
why you
absolutely need

someone

like

me.

* * *

Printed in the United States
90700LV00004B/33/A